Vintage Eyewear Style
1920s–1990s

Takano Fujii

Introduction

At the beginning of the twenty-first century, classic styles became the global trend in the eyeglass industry, and many brands and designers began to introduce new designs inspired by frames made decades ago. At the same time, the market for vintage eyeglasses grew and unique specialty stores sprang up in Japan. Never before has the wonderful design history of eyewear received so much attention in Japan.

This is the first book to describe vintage eyewear from 1920 to 1990, period by period. The eyeglass frames presented are neither from museum collections nor the collector's personal belongings. Vintage eyeglass shop staff and owners were interviewed and their wares photographed, with the resulting 131 valuable frames presented in full size in the pages to come. This means that many of these frames, with the exception of a few, can be seen in person and even purchased at stores.

The listings include gold-filled frames from the '20s with gorgeous engravings, French vintage from the '40s with beautiful celluloid luster, masterpieces from the '50s such as ARNEL and Wayfarer, and designer brands from the '60s and '70s such as Christian Dior and Pierre Cardin. Some classic models still hold up, even when viewed today, while others remain decorative, like jewelry. One thing is for certain: every frame is one of a kind and has a certain aura about it, and the historical fact that they were made from 25 years to a century ago is tantalizing.

In an age when it is easy to buy reasonably good-quality eyewear, choosing a vintage piece for your very own "special" look is a decadent pleasure. We hope that this book will prove a starting point for you to jump into the deep world of vintage eyeglasses.

Table of Contents

○ The information presented in this publication is current as of February 2021. Please note that it is based on interviews with specialty stores that cooperated with us as well as archival documents, but there may be slight differences in age and content.

○ How to read this book

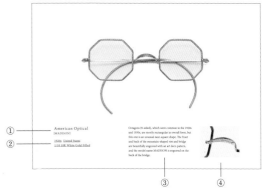

① American Optical
[MADISON]

② 1920s United States
1/10 10K White Gold Filled

Octagons (8-sided), which were common in the 1920s and 1930s, are mostly rectangular in overall form, but this one is an unusual near-square shape. The front and back of the mountain-shaped rim and bridge are beautifully engraved with an art deco pattern, and the model name MADISON is engraved on the back of the bridge.

①
Brand name
[Model name]
②
Age | Brand country
Frame material
③
Description
④
Enlarged detail

History of Eyewear

What started as a tool for correcting eyesight has evolved into an ornament and fashion accessory for personal expression and has now given rise to a culture of vintage enjoyment. First, let me tell you a bit about the history of how eyeglasses came to be what they are today.

Surprisingly, sunglasses came about before glasses to correct vision. In prehistoric times (before the third millennium BCE), Eskimos, blinded by strong sunlight reflecting off snow, cut slits into pieces of animal bone and hung them over their eyes. This new device, which was both a tool and an ornament, blocked out the glare and gave the Eskimos a more comfortable field of vision. Thus were the world's first sunglasses born. The true history of eyeglasses begins with lenses. In ancient times, humans learned to polish shiny surfaces for the purpose of concentrating sunlight to generate heat and life-giving fire. Lenses to correct human vision appeared in the first century BCE. It is written that the ancient Roman poet and philosopher Lucius Annaeus Seneca read books by enhanced light passed through a glass sphere filled with water. At about the same time, it was recorded that Emperor Nero, known as the tyrant of the Roman Empire, was known to have watched gladiatorial fights through emeralds, which seem to have served as sunglasses to protect his eyes from the bright glare of the sun. In the late 13th century, "spectacles for vision correction" finally made their appearance. There are various theories surrounding the emergence of eyeglasses, but it is believed that they originated between 1268 and 1289 in Florence or Venice, which boasted a flourishing glass industry. The world's first eyeglasses did not have temples, but rather two lenses fitted with a wooden frame in a pattern and connected by rivets. These "riveted glasses" were difficult to place on the nose and were typically held in the hand. Hence the modern form of glasses came about in the 13th century, but it would be some 450 years before a practical pair would arise.

Around 1727–30, London optician Edward Scarlett developed the first spectacles equipped with temples, the long stems of the frames that typically rest on the ears. They were probably fabricated from steel and had large rings at the ends of the temples that pressed against the head to hold the glasses in place. The invention was so revolutionary that

Tomain, the Queen of France's optician, wrote in 1746 of "spectacles with temples that allow easy breathing." Various other types appeared, including "finches," which were supported by a bridge across the nose; "lornettes," long-handled models used by ladies to watch the opera; and "single-sided glasses" that fit loosely into the eye socket and were favored by gentlemen. They were all forms of social ornamentation and largely served as symbols of wealth.

Practical eyeglasses with temples were manufactured in metal, tortoiseshell, and horn during the 18th and 19th centuries, but all were handmade by craftsmen, with only one produced at a time. As modernization progressed and demand for eyeglasses increased, it became necessary to rethink manufacturing methods.

The country that took the lead was not a European nation, but rather the United States. Founded in 1833, American Optical is the world's oldest surviving eyeglass manufacturer and played a major role in creating the epoch-making structures and designs that are now part of eyeglass history, as well as establishing a production system that helped popularize eyeglasses for the general public. For example, in 1843 they produced the first steel eyeglasses in the United States, in 1874 they invented the world's first rimless eyeglasses, and in 1885 they originated cable temples that curved behind the ear. The basic shape of eyeglasses began to be defined, and the 1920s marked the birth of a variety of eyewear styles.

Antique eyeglasses manufactured in the 1830s. The temples are sliding and retractable.

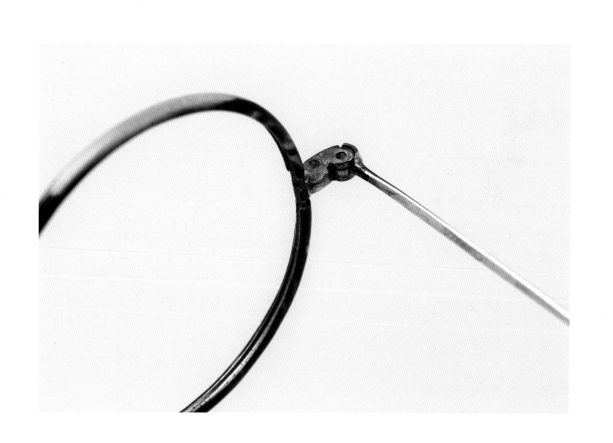

Parts & Features

1. rim: The frame that holds the lenses in place.

2. hinge: Hinges connect the front and temples.

3. temple: The vine-like parts that hang over the ears.

4. bridge: The part that bridges the gap between the left and right lenses.

5. nose pad: Parts that secure against the nose on both sides to prevent glasses from slipping off.

6. front: General term for the front part of the frame.

Start with the basic frame part names and detail highlights.
Knowing what to look for will open up the profound world of vintage eyeglasses.

 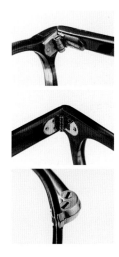  

Bridge and Nose Pads

Above: Saddle bridges without nose pads were common by the 1920s in Japan. *Middle*: Pads with clings still used today. *Bottom*: The pads on the plastic frames are made of a similar color material.

Hinge

Above: The method of attaching hinges on top of plastic frames is often seen in French vintage of the 1940s. *Middle*: Robust seven-barrel hinges to match the thick temples. *Bottom*: Dharma-shaped hinge with a rounded shape similar to a dharma doll.

Temple

Above: Cable temples, now rare, were created in 1885 for equestrian use. *Middle*: Celluloid fat temples, which retain their strength even without a core, were common in 1940s France. *Below*: The intricate carving by craftsmen is also exquisitely tasteful.

Rivet Decoration

Above & middle: The best part of 1950s and 1960s American vintage is the three-dimensional rivet decorations, such as diamond and cross-shaped rivets. *Below*: The type that attaches from the front with three pins is a traditional French vintage technique.

Frame Type

Round

This round lens shape became the prototype for today's eyeglasses. In the past, round lenses were fitted directly into the frame. The design is simple, has a strong presence, and creates a retro look when worn on the face.

Panto

A rounded inverted triangle, like an onigiri (rice ball) turned upside down. Also known as "P3" in the US and "Boston" in Japan. The one with the top corners up like a crown is called a "crown panto."

Square

This refers to a square lens shape. In Japan, the inverted trapezoidal shape with a wide top and bottom is called "Wellington" and has become a standard for classic frames. Shallow vertical sizes give a sharp look when hung on the face.

Teardrop

Slightly droopy lens shape in the shape of a water droplet. It was created in the 1930s as a shape that would not interfere with a pilot's oxygen mask. This is also known as an "aviator" or "eggplant type."

Here are the eight basic types of vintage eyeglass frames.
Be aware of the time period and background of the various lens shapes.

Cat's-Eye

The front ends are suspended like the eyes of a fox;
hence its name. When Marilyn Monroe wore it on
screen in the '50s it became a worldwide phenomenon.

Oval

This popular shape is a horizontal oval. Its character-
istic feature is its flowing lines, which create a gentle
atmosphere when worn. When smaller frames became
the trend in the 1990s, many variations appeared.

Sirmont

Model with a metal bridge dividing the left and right plastic
brow.
The name "Sir Mont" comes from the fact that in the
1950s an American military officer by the name of
Mont ordered a pair of "dignified" eyeglasses.

Polygon

The polygonal shape is a classic shape seen from the
early vintage era of the 1920s. They come in varying types, such as hexagons (six-sided) and octagons
(eight-sided), and when worn project an intellectual air.

Material Type

Celluloid

The world's first plastic, synthesized from cellulose (nitrocellulose) and camphor. It has good coloring, is sturdy, and can be used to create free-form patterns, but it is easily ignited and difficult to handle. Currently it is not widely used.

Zyl

Zyl, or Zylonite, is an expression that was in limited use until about the 1950s, before the term "plastic" became widespread. It is made from nitrocellulose cotton, and in the United States plastic in general is sometimes called Zyl.

Acetate

Made from a compound of nitrocellulose and acetic acid, this material is now the main component of plastic frames. It has a beautiful luster and transparent coloring and is easily adjustable for temples and other parts because it bends with heat.

Optyl

Developed by Austrian scientist Wilhelm Unger in 1964. It is made from epoxy resin and has beautiful colors and luster. This lightweight material can express complex shapes and is resistant to aging.

Materials for eyeglasses can be broadly classified into plastic and metal. In the case of vintage, some rare materials are not in use today.

Gold-Filled

These were made by stretching a gold plate over the core material. In English it is Gold Filled (GF), and "1/10 12KGF" refers to one-tenth the thickness of 12-karat gold. This is opposed to gold plating, which is a thin gold film attached to the surface.

Aluminum

A light, rust-resistant, corrosion-resistant metal used for coins and drinking-water cans. With its metallic texture and futuristic atmosphere, it attracted attention as a new material for eyeglasses in the 1950s and 1960s.

Solid Gold

This means pure gold. Originally 24-karat gold was used to indicate unmixed gold, but 18-karat and 14-karat gold mixed with certain metals to increase strength are also sometimes referred to as solid gold. Solid-gold glasses were widely distributed in Japan during its "bubble economy" (1986–1991).

Nickel Alloy

An alloy of nickel with other metal, such as copper or chromium. It has long been widely used as a material for metal frames because of its excellent corrosion resistance, heat resistance, and ease of processing.

Chapter 1

In the early 1920s, nose pads did not yet exist for eyeglasses, and a saddle bridge that followed the shape of the nose was set with cable temples that hooked behind the ears. Lens shapes were mainly round, and the temples were of the "side-mount" style, leading from the center of the front. In the midst of all this, when American Optical developed nose pads in 1923 the bridge was freed from the function of a nose pad, and a freer design was born. It was also a time when the demand and production of jewelry was drastically decreasing due to World War I. Jewelry makers who had lost their jobs entered the eyeglass industry and began to apply decorative engraving to their frames. Gold-filled, in which thick sheets of gold are wrapped around base metal, was often used as the material for frames. At this time the US was offering tax incentives for gold products as part of its export promotion measures, and these factors, coupled with the current climate, led to gold-filled frames with artistic engravings that swept from the US to the European market as well.

At the same time, the Hollywood film industry was entering its golden age. Comedic actor Harold Lloyd appeared on numerous screens wearing plastic round glasses. The prompt, suit-clad "glass character" gained popularity and became so dominant that his round glasses were called "Lloyd's Glasses." It was so influential that it ushered in a round-glasses boom in Japan and became the first pair of glasses used commercially in the film industry.

1920s

Gold-Filled Frames and "Lloyd's Glasses"

American Optical

<u>1920s</u>, <u>United States</u>
<u>1/10 10K White Gold Filled</u>

The design is representative of the '20s, with a saddle bridge without nose pad, a round shape close to a regular circle, and cable temples that wrap around behind the ears. The metal rim is mountain shaped in cross section, with delicate geometric engravings on the front and back surfaces.

Unknown

1920s, France
14K Gold-Filled Zyl

A round shape with 14k gold-filled frames and clear yellow rims. The rim of the Zyl material retains its strength even without a core, and the transparency of the material is more pronounced. They are made using a manufacturing method that is rare today, in which metal parts grip plastic rims.

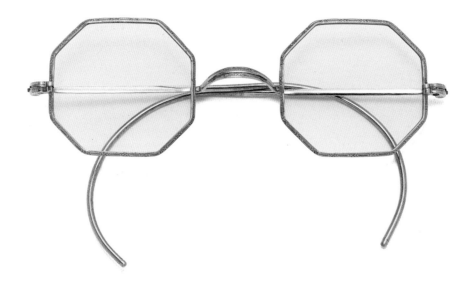

American Optical
[MADISON]

1920s, United States
1/10 10K White Gold Filled

Octagons (eight-sided), which were common in the 1920s and 1930s, are mostly rectangular in overall form, but this one is an unusual near-square shape. The front and back of the mountain-shaped rim and bridge are beautifully engraved with an art deco pattern, and the model name MADISON is engraved on the back of the bridge.

Unknown

1920s, France
Gold-Filled Celluloid

The retro true circle round shape is a celluloid wrapped type with a thin tortoiseshell-patterned celluloid wrapped around a gold-filled metal rim. The saddle bridge, which has no nose pads, is a rare specification with cellular affixed to the part of the bridge that touches the nose for comfort.

Unknown

1920s, United States
1/10 12K White Gold Filled
10K Solid Gold

Round shape with "side-mount"-style temples leading from right beside the front. The 12-karat gold-filled frames are gorgeous, with geometric patterns on the front and back of the rims and leaflike engravings on the upper surface. The nose pad was created in 1923, and this pad is solid gold.

Unknown

1920s, United States
Zyl

Combination type with tortoiseshell-pattern plastic rims and heavy design metal bridges. The rims are sandwiched between round, three-dimensional, engraved metal parts—a unique manufacturing method—and the temples have a flat shape that lies on its side.

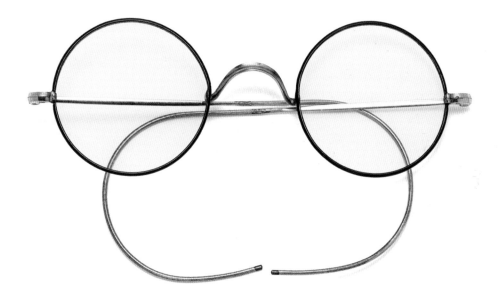

Unknown

<u>1920s</u>, <u>France</u>
<u>Gold Filled</u>

The round shape with dark-brown rim looks at first glance like "celluloid" wrapped in plastic, but in fact it is an unusual specification with cloisonné applied to the metal. The bridge, which protrudes forward, has a flowing form with a hollowed inner side that shows the high level of processing technology at the time.

American Optical
[CORTLAND]

1920s, United States
1/10 12K White Gold Filled
10K Solid Gold

Around the '20s and '30s, American Optical frames had model names determined by the design of the bridge. "CORTLAND," with its rounded U-shaped bridge, is a representative model, and there are many different materials and ball shapes depending on the period. The frame is gold lined and the nose pads are solid gold.

Unknown

1920s, United Kingdom
Tortoiseshell, Gold Filled

Vintage frames made in England with a warm, genuine tortoiseshell front and extremely thin gold-filled cable temples. The lenses are round in shape but the front is a rounded rhombus; this subtle difference accentuates the design.

SAKURA OPTICAL

1920s, Japan
Celluloid, Chrome Plating

A celluloid-wrapped round shape made in Tokyo during the Taisho era (1912–26). Thin black celluloid is wrapped around the saddle bridge, as well as the metal rim, and the cable temples are plated black. The chic texture enhances the monotone and simple design.

Unknown

1920s, France
Tortoiseshell

Simple round glasses in deep-dark-brown genuine tortoiseshell with long, thin, straight temples catch the eye. The hinges are not dug in and embedded but are placed on the material and firmly attached, a process unique to tortoiseshell glasses.

BECK
[ROCKGLAS]

1920s, United States
Steel

Sunglasses for driving began to become popular in the '20s. ROCKGLAS, used by the US Air Force and Army, has a movable bridge section that follows the shape of the face. The droplet shape was once called "auto-shaped" in Japan, but it is thought that the term originated from these automobile sunglasses.

BAY STATE OPTICAL
[PRINCETON]

1920s, United States
Zyl

The first plastic-framed round glasses from
the same period as the "Lloyd glasses" (round
glasses) that were the trademark of Harold Lloyd,
a leading comedian in the '20s. It is made of
highly transparent Zyl that imitates tortoiseshell,
and its flowing form is thought to have been
manufactured by injection molding.

American Optical

1920s, United States
White Gold Filled

Its shape is a small octagon. The rims and bridges are engraved with "milled" engraving, in which small round grains are stamped by skilled craftsmen. The temple ends are a hollow design of thin metal folded to prevent the glasses from slipping down, while also serving to reduce weight.

Unknown

<u>1920s</u>, <u>France</u>
<u>14K Gold Filled</u>

This rimless round shape was manufactured in France. Most glasses with temples in the '20s had saddle bridges without nose pads, but this one has a keyhole-shaped bridge commonly used for finch glasses. It is a rare design that also features a thin nose pad.

Unknown

1920s, United States
1/10 12K White Gold Filled
10K Solid Gold

Octagonal shape with a novel polygonal bridge with raised edges. The 12-karat gold-filled frames are luxuriously finished with engraving on three sides: front, back, and top of the rim. The intricate engravings, which are done by hand by skilled craftsmen, have a unique depth of flavor that is difficult to reproduce with modern technology.

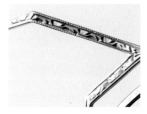

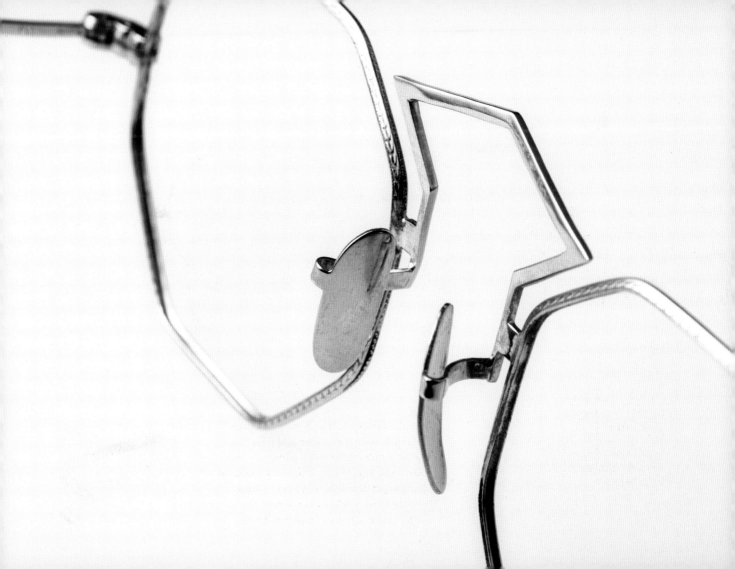

Chapter 2

A major evolution in the construction of eyeglasses occurred in the 1930s. Most eyeglasses up to that time had the base of the temples directly next to the lens, but in 1930 American Optical developed and patented "FUL-VUE," which pushed the position of the temples upward. This allowed the temples to provide a wider field of vision without obstructing the view. At the same time, the lens could be tilted to the side of the face to provide a more comfortable field of vision and fit the contours of the face. It is said that the Panto lens shape was created by raising the position of the temples and the upper front portion protruding to the side. Rimless glasses were also evolving. To secure the exposed lens while protecting it, American Optical developed the Numont, which consists of a plate spring stacked on the side of a glass lens and fastened

at a single point. The "RIMWAY" that followed succeeded in preventing lens misalignment and breakage by fastening the lens in two places and flapping the metal rim.

In addition, until the 1930s sunglasses were mostly goggle type, designed for motorcycles and industrial safety, but the development of pilot's glasses progressed as World War II began in earnest. At the request of the US Army Air Corps, Bausch&Lomb developed the teardrop-type "aviator," and Ray-Ban was born in 1937. In Europe the "RATTI" company, which supplied goggles to the Italian air force, founded Persol in 1938. Thus, the '30s was a time of shift to eyewear that emphasized functionality and durability.

1930s

Evolution from "FUL-VUE"

American Optical
[FUL-VUE]

1930s, United States
1/10 12K Gold-Filled Bakelite

The FUL-VUE style, which uses temples that connect from the top of the front, was created in 1930, when automobiles first became popular in the United States, to provide a wide field of vision. American Optical patented this structure, and other brands paid a licensing fee to adopt FUL-VUE.

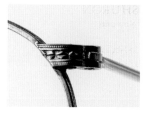

SHURON
[Numont]

1930s, United States
1/10 12K Gold Filled

The Numont eyeglass model entails fastening a rimless frame at a single point on each lens, allowing the load to be absorbed by three plate springs on the sides of the lens and crawling metal rims. Numont stands for "New Mounting = new lens mounting method," and this structure has drastically reduced the breakage of glass lenses in rimless systems.

Bausch&Lomb
[Numont]

1930s, United States
1/10 12K Gold-Filled Bakelite

Rimless frames connected by a bar bridge manufactured by Bausch&Lomb. Although it used a Numont-style fastening at a single point on the lens, this structure was originally conceived of by American Optical. Since the trademark was not registered, many brands launched frames with the same structure and name.

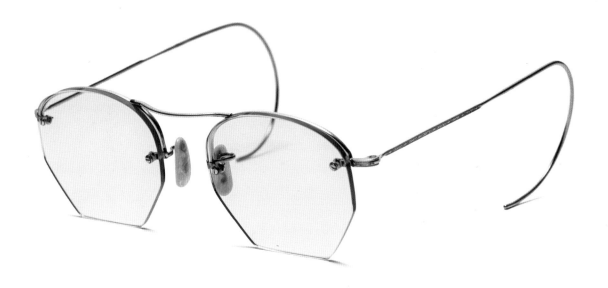

G&W OPTICAL
[RIMWAY FUL-VUE]

1930s, United States
1/10 12K White-Gold-Filled
Bakelite

The "RIM WAY," in which the left and right sides of the lens of a rimless frame are fixed at two points and a metal bar is placed along the top of the lens, is a universal style that has been adopted in many current eyewear products. Since the lens is fixed at two points, there is less load on the lens, and the metal bar also serves as a design accent.

American Optical
[FUL-VUE SAFETY SPECTACLE]

1930s, United States
Stainless Steel

The "FUL-VUE" style with cable temples is actually safety glasses (protective eyewear) designed to protect the eyes at worksites. The sturdy, thick stainless steel used for the frames and the lack of engraving on the rims are because the frame focuses on function rather than decoration.

Unknown

1930s, France
Nickel Alloy, Celluloid
Bakelite

"FUL-VUE," which became very popular in the US in the 1930s, was also adopted in France. The celluloid-wrapped Panto, made of tortoiseshell-patterned celluloid, features a bridge that is curved on both edges instead of being flat. The French interpretation of FUL-VUE, which is slightly different from the American one, is unique.

Unknown

<u>1930s</u>, <u>France</u>
<u>Nickel Alloy</u>, <u>Celluloid</u>
<u>Bakelite</u>

The celluloid-wrapped, which incorporates the "FUL-VUE" style, looks round at first glance but actually has a French spirit, in that it is egg shaped. The nose pad material was Bakelite, a phenolic resin introduced in 1909.

Unknown

1930s, France
Plastic

Injection-molded frames from the dawn of plastic eyeglasses in France. The rounded lens shape and the cat's-ear-like form are unique. The thick, fat temples feature no core and are made of robust five-barrel hinges.

OPTIKS

1930s, United States
Plastic

These are injection-molded plastic frames manufactured in the United States. The inverted-triangle Panto shape has a clear yellow front and clear brown ultrathick temples, each with a dot pattern around the edge. It is a simple yet highly decorative piece.

Unknown

1930s, United Kingdom
Plastic

Tortoiseshell-patterned plastic frames
manufactured by handmade machining. The
wide temples have no core and sturdy five-
barrel hinges. The front is attached by two
pins and the temples by three pins, and the
rounded, note-like temple ends are a design
often seen in British products of the 1930s.

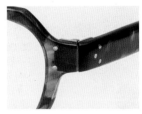

American Optical
[Spectacle Goggle]

1930s, United States
Stainless Steel

Motorcycle goggles with thick, flat glass lenses. The front is made of strong stainless steel, and the sides have leather windshields for wind and dust protection. The cable temples are wrapped with a transparent cover to prevent them from slipping off due to impact or other reasons.

RATTI OPTICAL
INDUSTRIES SOCIETY
[PROTECTOR]

1930s, Italy
Resin

Goggle sunglasses with side guards manufactured by "RATTI," the predecessor of the Italian sunglass brand Persol, founded in 1938. Made of lightweight resin material, the high-curved frames are worn to keep the windshield firmly in place on the face, to guard against wind and dust.

Chapter 3

After World War II, sunglasses quickly spread among the general public. The teardrop "aviators" adopted by the US military not only looked cool but were also popular with the average person due to their connection to the military. At the time, the pilot was considered the modern version of a knight in shining armor, and wearing "aviators" was a sign of patriotism. Worn by General Douglas MacArthur and others, its popularity spread throughout the world, and a large number of variations were manufactured. And so the teardrop would remain the original form of sunglasses to this day.

During the war, the use of gold was restricted to compensate for the shortage of supplies, and the production of gold-filled frames decreased. Around the world, plastic was developed as an alternative. In the postwar period the supply of goods became stable, and glasses made of celluloid and similar materials, which are easy to color, could be mass-produced, and the glasses material gradually shifted from metal to plastic. At the same time, decorative combs were beginning to decline, but combmakers had already switched from tortoiseshell and horn to celluloid, and skilled craftsmen began to turn their talents to eyewear. The manufacture of celluloid eyewear then became active in Leminster, Massachusetts, and in the Jura region of France, which used traditional techniques. The quality of French celluloid in the 1940s was particularly high, and many beautiful frames with a unique luster were produced during this period.

1940s

Pilot's Glasses and Celluloid

Unknown
[The rock]

1940s, France
Celluloid

The '40s was the golden age of French vintage. The celluloid fabric of the time had a wet, shiny, and bewitching texture, and the multifaceted cut created an unforgettable and original lens shape. The temples are also cut in a three-dimensional manner to fit the face.

Unknown
[Marcel]

1940s, France
Celluloid

Oversized square shape like a "mask" with a celluloid fabric surface. The front is attached with three-point pins, using a traditional French manufacturing method. The straight temples are made of solid celluloid, which is strong enough to maintain its strength even without a core.

Unknown
[Rubik]

1940s, France
Celluloid

The upper rim is angled, while the lower rim is rounded. The exquisite balance of straight and curved lines is unique and looks great on the honey-amber celluloid fabric, which is as beautiful as candy. As in the manufacturing process of tortoiseshell glasses, the hinges are attached on top of the fabric without a counterbore on the frame.

Unknown
[Night ranger]

1940s, France
Celluloid

Avant-garde design with a straight brow line that drops abruptly at an angle toward the bridge. The contrast between the extreme angularity of the front and the smooth cutting of the extra-thick fat temples is unique. It is a powerful form that cannot be expressed by mass production.

Unknown
[bowser]

1940s, France
Celluloid

The combination of a strong front with an extreme mountain-like lift and the transparent and soft impression of honey tortoiseshell celluloid is unique. The nose pads are thinly shaved and made of a material that is the same color as the frame, and the coreless fat temples are comfortable on the skin.

Unknown

1940s, France
Celluloid

The Crown Panto, with its crown-like top corners, sparked the current French vintage boom. Iconic details include the voluminous 8 mm thick celluloid, edgy cutting, three-pin attachment, and coreless fat temples.

Unknown

<u>1940s</u>, <u>France</u>
<u>Celluloid</u>

The orthodox Panto is made of a rose-colored clear type of material. The rim is designed to be slightly narrower than most of the French vintage of the '40s, but the three-dimensional bridge gives it a fairly rare finish. The wide, coreless celluloid temples are highly transparent and look sleek when worn.

American Optical

1940s, United States
Zyl

Eyewear made of Zyl material increased in production after World War II. The two-tone square shape, made of two different materials pasted together, has a luxurious aesthetic with a shimmering pearlescent look. The detailing is elaborate, with the bridge stepped down from the front.

Bausch&Lomb
[Aristocrat]

1940s–50s, United States
1/10 12K Gold Filled

Around the mid-1940s the "bar bridge" model with a single-line bridge placed high became more numerous. It was a powerful design that was a departure from the saddle bridge models without nose pads, which had been the mainstream style until then, but matched the rounded, rimless, square shape.

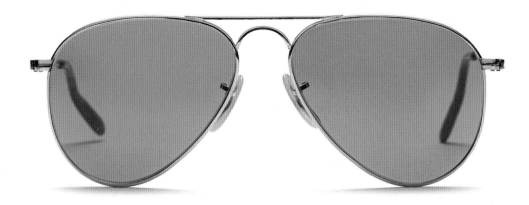

SHURON
[FUL-VUE]

1940s, United States
1/10 12K Gold Filled

Pilot sunglasses created by SHURON, a long-established American brand founded in 1865. The teardrop, which combines a double bridge with a droplet lens shape that allows for a wide field of vision, is a classic in sunglass design and remains popular to this day. The back of the bridge is engraved "FUL-VUE."

American Optical
[Pilot Glasses]

1940s, United States
1/10 12K Gold Filled

In the '40s, American Optical was one of the US Air Force's designated suppliers of glasses for jet fighter pilots. The straight temples, which can be taken on and off while wearing a helmet, and the robust thick double bridge are all specified by the US Air Force.

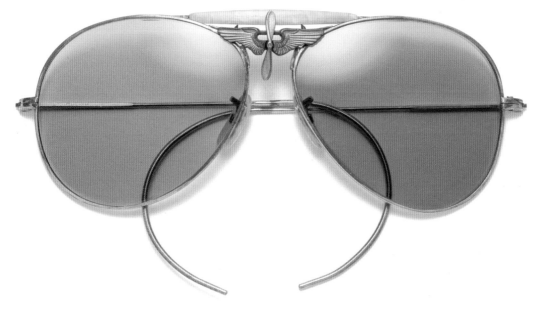

ART CRAFT
[WWII BALD-EAGLE
US AIR FORCE AVIATOR]

1940s, United States
1/10 12K Gold Filled

In the center of the frame is a propeller and the
wing of a bald eagle, the national bird of the
United States. The design is actually a symbol of
the US Air Force, and these may be the sunglasses
that were issued to officers of higher ranks during
World War II. It is a powerful teardrop that evokes
the mood of the times.

American Optical
[FUL-VUE SHOOTER]

1940s, United States
1/10 12K Gold-Filled
Bakelite

These sunglasses are designed for hunting and shooting, featuring a brow bar to keep sweat from flowing and an extremely narrow bridge. The lenses are in American Optical's proprietary green lens color called "CALOBAR," and the brow bars and cable-type temples are made of Bakelite.

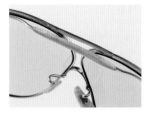

FLIGHT

<u>1940s</u>, <u>United States</u>
<u>Gold Plated</u>

Eye-catching pilot sunglasses with a downward-curving sweatproof brow bar and extremely raised lens shape. It was manufactured by VISION PRODUCTS and has "FLIGHT" engraved on the top of the metal bridge.

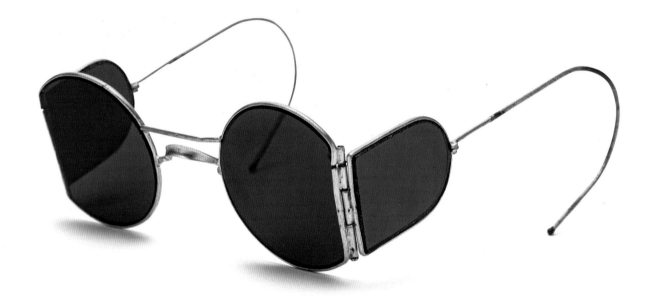

Unknown

1940s, Soviet Union
Stainless Steel

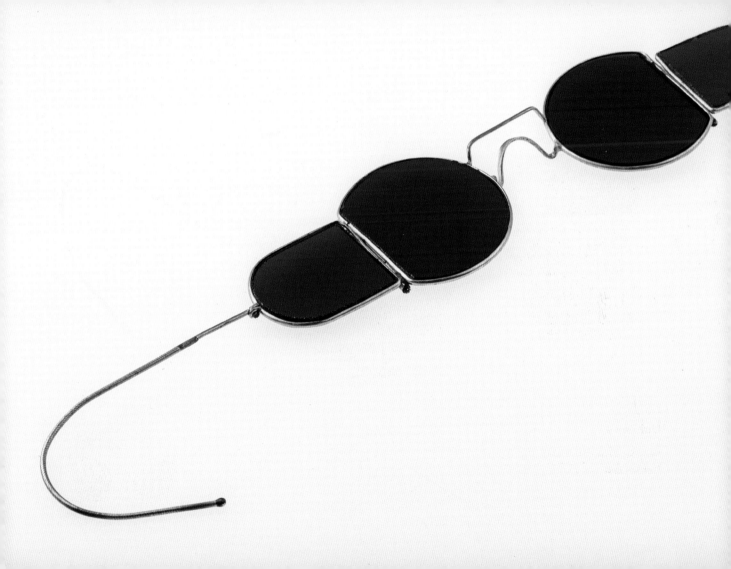

The golden age of American vintage was the 1950s. During this period, plastic-processing technology improved dramatically, making possible a wide variety of designs and colors and leading to the birth of many legendary models. The most representative example is TART OPTICAL's ARNEL. The rugged design of the nearly square shape with diamond-shaped decorative rivets was a favorite of James Dean, and a look later imitated by Johnny Depp, well known for often sporting them. In 1953 Ray-Ban's Wayfarer, a masterpiece in the history of sunglasses, came on to the scene. These sharp square sunglasses are still in use more than half a century later. In similar fashion, American Optical released SARATOGA, known to have been a favorite of John F. Kennedy. The '50s saw the appearance of many square shapes with decorative rivets, and everyone from East Coast jazzmen to West Coast Hollywood stars became obsessed with them.

The brow-type Sirmont, which truly represented the '50s, also exploded in popularity in the United States. The roots can be traced to the late '40s, when Jack Rohrbach, a frame engineer at SHURON, adopted a plastic brow as a method to reduce the use of gold by 50% at a time when gold prices were soaring. Marilyn Monroe also wore a cat's-eye shape with the sides lifted up in the 1953 film *How to Marry a Millionaire*, which led to a craving for this shape among women. The '50s was also the period when the standard vintage frame design was established.

1950s

The Golden Age of American Vintage

TART OPTICAL
[ARNEL]

1950s, United States
Zyl

TART OPTICAL's ARNEL was a favorite of Johnny Depp and sparked the vintage eyeglasses boom. It features a square shape with a nearly 1:1 aspect ratio, diamond-shaped decorative rivets, and solid seven-barrel hinges. The rough finish, such as the misalignment of the temple joints, is rather tasteful.

TART OPTICAL
[BRYAN]

<u>1950s</u>, <u>United States</u>
<u>Zyl</u>

TART OPTICAL's BRYAN is a popular model favored by Woody Allen, and several different rivet designs exist. This is a type with a change in decorative rivets, with diamond-shaped rivets on the front, crown-shaped rivets on the temples, and seven-barrel hinges on the thicker temples.

Ray-Ban
[Wayfarer]

1950s, United States
Zyl

The first model of Ray-Ban's legendary Wayfarer, created in 1953. The unique style, with the side of the sunglasses lifted up and the thin temples, point to it being of the first generation. From the second generation, released in 1961, to the present, Wayfarers have thick temples that curve around the ear.

American Optical
[SARATOGA]

1950s, United States
Zyl

Once a favorite of John F. Kennedy, the SARATOGA is a standard design that symbolizes the United States of America. Slightly slender for the '50s, they feature a raised square shape with diamond-shaped rivets, and the Calobar engraved on the frame refers to the green lens color.

Bausch&Lomb
[SAFETY]

1950s, United States
Zyl

Safety glass in a clear pink square shape with cross decorative rivets and covered cable temples. The translucent light-pink color was called "Flesh" at the time and was very familiar to the face; it became an underground favorite in the US and Europe in the 1950s.

Bausch&Lomb
[SAFETY]

1950s, United States
Acetate

While blue-collar workers used protective glasses with wind guards at the time, the white-collar elite wore glasses with decorative rivets, as if to display their status. These were called "VIP Safety" (safety glasses for the VIP class) with a hint of irony.

TITMUS

1950s, United States
Acetate

These are the "original safety glasses" worn by blue-collar workers to protect their eyes while working. A mesh wind guard is fitted to prevent dust and iron particles from entering through gaps. The temples are stamped "Z87," indicating that they meet US safety standards.

TART OPTICAL
[F.D.R]

1950s, United States
Zyl

The initials of President Franklin Delano Roosevelt were the origin of the model name. The frames have a strong design with thick, straight lines and three-point rivets on the front and temples. This model was a favorite of actor Cary Grant and jazz musician Yusef Lateef.

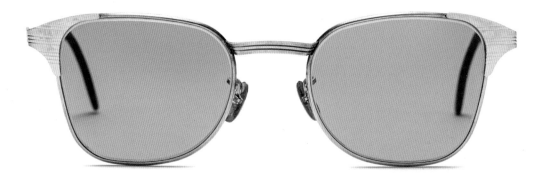

Bausch&Lomb
[Signet]

1950s, United States
1/10 12K Gold Filled

In America of the 1950s, "Speed Line" linear designs were used in many automobiles, home appliances, and other products, as if to reflect expectations for the future. This was also true of the eyewear of the time, which was decorated with strong, fast-moving lines from the front side to the temples.

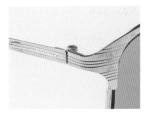

Ray-Ban

<u>1950s</u>, <u>United States</u>
<u>1/10 12K Gold Filled</u>

Ray-Ban was launched in 1937 by
Bausch&Lomb. A representative model is the
droplet-shaped "aviator" type of sunglasses.
The temple ends were made of Bakelite in
the '40s and later clear plastic in the '50s. The
bridge is stamped "B&L RAY-BAN U.S.A."

American Optical

1950s, United States
Acetate, 1/10 12K Gold Filled

The Sirmont, which combines a metal bridge with a plastic brow, is an American style representative of the 1950s known as Malcolm X's preferred glasses. The decorative rivets with arrow marks and temples with varying thicknesses are the same design as the model he used.

Bausch&Lomb
[BAL RIM]

1950s, United States
Zyl, 1/10 12K Gold Filled

Combination model of a Sirmont brow type with cable temples. It is characterized by heavy, three-dimensional rivet decoration and edgy cutting. The model name BAL-RIM comes from the initials of Bausch&Lomb, and there exist several different colors and temple variations.

STYL-RITE OPTICS
[DOBBS]

1950s, United States
Zyl, 1/10 12K Gold Filled

Sirmont, which uses redwood Zyl material, a coloring unique to the '50s in the United States. It features a rounded, soft brow line and front, and the 12-karat gold-filled metal bridge and rims are graceful and luxurious.

American Optical
[SHOW TIME]

1950s, United States
Zyl, 1/10 12K Gold Filled

The cat's-eye shape with raised sides was very popular in the 1950s because it "made women look intelligent and sexy." Named SHOW TIME, this model has an elegant finish with gorgeous bridge engraving, three-dimensional rivets, and the use of an elegant pearlescent brown color.

Unknown

1950s, France
Celluloid

The cat's-eyes, which became popular in the
United States in the 1950s, were also adopted
in France around the same time. This piece is
made of voluminous celluloid, has a thickness of
8 mm, and boasts decorative studs—a rarity in
French vintage. These glasses are carefully crafted,
including hinges that have been flattened by
dropping the heads of the pins.

SHURON

1950s, United States
1/10 12K Gold Filled
Aluminum, Acetate

Brow-type cat's-eye-shaped glasses. The brow bar is made of acetate and the temples are aluminum, a new material at the time. These are elegant and gorgeous designs in flamboyant pearl blue and beautiful shiny silver colors, which create a feminine look.

Chapter 5

Certain events that symbolize the 1960s include the Beatles, miniskirts (which were all the rage), the birth of hippie culture, and the successful Apollo 11 moon landing. During this period of drastic cultural and value changes, eyewear also evolved by ravenously absorbing fashion and art trends. A prominent example is the rise of French designer brands such as LAN-VIN, pierre cardin, courrèges, and Christian Dior. At that time, eyewear as a fashionable item had not yet been established, and designers were free to create extreme shapes, such as round and square, asymmetrical forms, and ornate decorations. The 1960s was also a time when the space race between the US and the Soviet Union was heating up. People had a longing for space, and elements of the space age were incorporated into many products of the time. In the case of eyeglasses, aluminum with a metallic texture was often used as a new material. The influence of pop art could also be seen. Colorful and bright hues by artists such as Andy Warhol and Roy Lichtenstein were also actively used in frames.

OLIVER GOLDSMITH, founded in 1926, also created a stir in the conservative British eyewear scene. Around the 1960s the company introduced many big-shape sunglasses and frames with bold cuts favored by icons of the era, such as Audrey Hepburn and Michael Caine. The 1960s was a time when eyewear design blossomed and refined at a rapid pace, with free ideas.

1960s

The Rise of Luxury Brands

LANVIN
by PHILIPPE CHEVALLIER

1960s, France
Acetate

LANVIN sunglasses by eyewear designer Philippe Chevalier. It is a novel design in which temples divided into two halves are connected at the tips, and four special parts called "wrapped front-end hinges" that open 180 degrees are used. The big shape that covers the face is a silhouette that symbolizes the '60s.

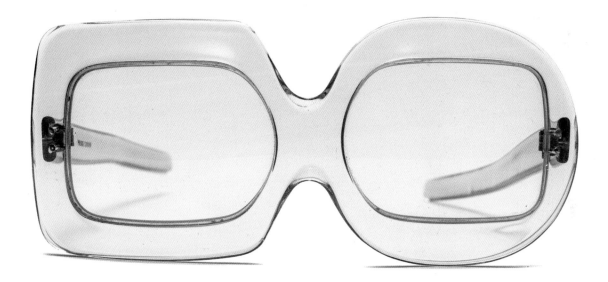

pierre cardin

1960s, France
Plastic

Asymmetrical sunglasses combining "round" and "square." It is a futuristic design that symbolizes the mood of "space-age longing" in the 1960s. The use of a clear blue material with high transparency emphasizes the futuristic feel of the product.

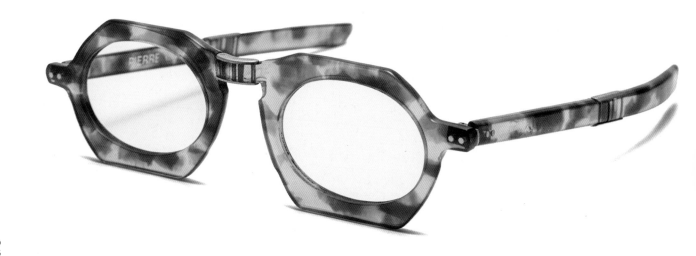

pierre cardin

1960s, France
Plastic

This folding style is Pierre Cardin's signature work. Fold the front inward and then fold it up, so that it hugs from the temples for compactness. The octagonal front is matched with oval lenses, and the transparent honey tortoiseshell creates a sense of luxury.

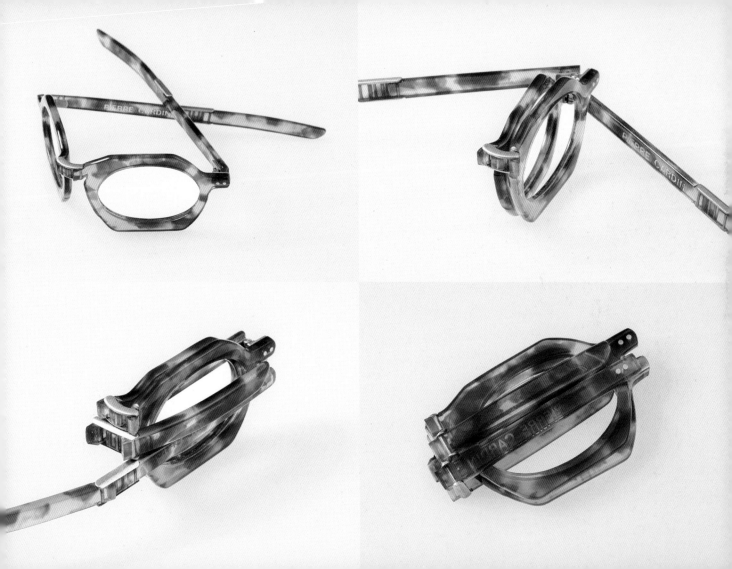

pierre cardin

1960s, France
Plastic

Folding style with a large round front and
square lens shape. The temples are placed
vertically from the front so that the vines do
not overlap when folded. The asymmetry of
the design adds to its uniqueness.

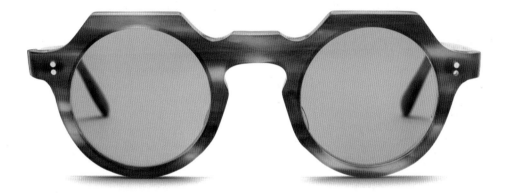

Unknown

<u>1960s</u>, <u>France</u>
<u>Acetate</u>

This is a smaller-sized model among the "crown panto," one of the traditional French eyeglass designs, with a unique round shape closer to a regular circle, and is cut with raised edges. The temples, slender for French vintage, have a metal core for strength.

courrèges
[eskimo]

<u>1960s</u>, <u>France</u>
<u>Plastic</u>

The design, in which the majority of the lenses are covered by the frame, pays homage to the "original sunglasses," which were once worn by Inuit, who cut slits into animal bone and used them to protect their eyes from the reflection of snow. This iconic piece graced the cover of *Vogue* in the 1960s.

OLIVER GOLDSMITH

1960s, United Kingdom
Unknown

The square shape was created by the British brand OLIVER GOLDSMITH, founded in 1926. The frames are heavy, with an ebony-like texture, and the edgy cut of the brow line and ultrathick straight temples are quite eye-catching. The owllike appearance is unique.

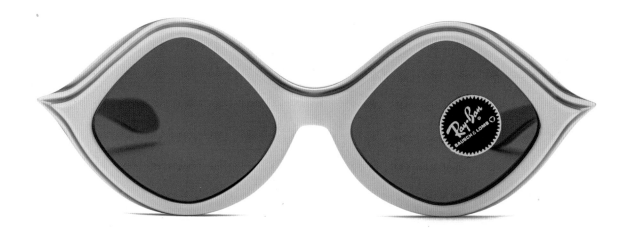

Ray-Ban
[TAMARIN]

1960s, United States
Acetate

Although basic designs are the mainstream mission of Ray-Ban, the company introduced these innovative frames in the late 1960s. The unique lens shape is a rhombus with a futuristic design of layered off-white and blue lines. The model name TAMARIN refers to a monkey that lives in Central and South America.

Ray-Ban
[CARAVAN]

1960s, United States
1/10 12K Gold Filled

CARAVAN, created in 1957, is a popular model embodying the Ray-Ban style with its square shape and double-bridge style. This one has a special silver mirror lens, and only the lower part of the lens is clear, to allow the pilot better visibility in the cockpit.

STYL-RITE OPTICS

1960s, United States
Aluminum
1/40 10K Rolled Gold Plated

Aluminum became very popular in the 1960s as a new material for eyeglass frames. It is characterized by lightness and rust resistance and boasts a much-longer life span than gold-filled. The brow type, which gained popularity in the '50s, also incorporated aluminum later in the '60s, adding a space-age element.

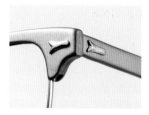

MARINE

1960s, United States
Zyl, Aluminum

The square shape, the standard in the US of the 1950s, was combined with aluminum temples, a new material at the time. The aluminum temples are stepped down and embellished with elaborate details, such as matching riveted decorations of different square and trapezoidal shapes.

Bausch&Lomb

1960s, United States
Zyl

This unusual design features a voluminous square shape with a hollowed-out double bridge and cross-shaped decorative rivets. The "Z87" engraved on the back of the temples is an indication the glasses meet American industrial standards. Impact-resistant lenses can be fitted with these glasses.

Persol

<u>1960s,</u> <u>Italy</u>
<u>Acetate</u>

Persol high-curve sunglasses manufactured by RATTI. The temples are equipped with "MEFLECT," an original mechanism that enhances springiness. The brown glass lenses are the brand's iconic color and match the brown wooden frames.

AUGUSTA GAGET

<u>1960s</u>, <u>France</u>
<u>Acetate</u>, <u>Rhinestone</u>

Created by eyewear designer Augusta Gadget, this decorative piece symbolizes the mood of Paris in the late 1960s. The fluttering butterflies are encrusted with colorful rhinestones, and the large frames, which protrude from the face, resemble Venetian masks.

Christian Dior

1960s, France
1/10 12K Gold Filled

OPTIQUE MAGNIFIQUE
[4319]

1960s, United States
Zyl

These iconic round glasses were a favorite of architect Le Corbusier. Manufactured in France and sold by an American brand, the voluminous round shape is decorated with hexagonal star-shaped pin ornaments. Straight, fat temples are another one of its trademarks.

OLIVER GOLDSMITH
[ZOOK]

1960s, United Kingdom
Acetate

The square-shaped ZOOK has a diagonal television cut around the lens, calling to mind cathode ray tube televisions to create a three-dimensional effect and reduce weight. OLIVER GOLDSMITH in the 1960s was made in England, but labor-intensive methods such as these "television cuts" were manufactured in France.

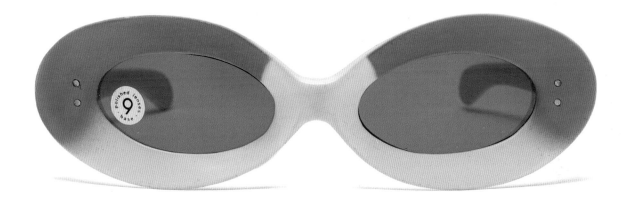

Unknown

<u>1960s</u>, <u>Italy</u>
<u>Acetate</u>

These oval-shaped sunglasses made in Italy pose a vivid contrast of turquoise blue and off-white. The bold "television cut" on the front creates depth when viewed from the side. The original glass lenses impart a sense of luxury.

Unknown

1960s, France
Acetate, Gold Filled

The combination of a metal brow bar
with a dangling acetate rim is the "amor"
style, popular in '50s and '60s France. The
combination of the two-tone front with
tortoiseshell pattern and clear and gold
metal brow give it a dignified yet intellectual
appearance.

OLIVER GOLDSMITH
[KOKO]

1960s, United Kingdom
Acetate

This glamorous pair from OLIVER GOLDSMITH is their answer to the big-shape round sunglasses that were all the rage in the '60s. For the front, thick acetate was carved to create a sculptural, three-dimensional form. The high quality of the glass lenses is reflected in the fresh white frames.

Unknown

1960s, France
Acetate, Crystal

During the 1960s and 1970s, opticians in the Jura region of France crafted artistic frames to show off their masterful skills. While the hand-embedded crystals are a masterpiece, the intricate frames have been painstakingly polished, displaying the pride the craftsmen have in their work.

Chapter 6

In the 1970s, many big shapes and complex forms that covered the face appeared, especially among sunglasses. One of the reasons for this was the adoption of new materials. Developed by Austrian scientist Wilhelm Unger, Optyl is a resinous material that can more fully express beautiful colors, gloss, and patterns. Its characteristics are its extremely light weight, resistance to deterioration over time, and luxurious texture. The '70s saw the introduction of Christian Dior and Dunhill's Optyl collections, which led to a reduction in the weight of large frames. Sunglasses at this time became a good item to raise the brand's profile, and as time progressed the logo engraved on the inside of the temples began to display more prominently on the outside. Also, while glass lenses were the norm until the 1960s, the 1970s saw a gradual shift to plastic lenses, which are lighter and easier to process. Plastic lenses were able to accommodate larger frames, which also assisted the big-shape trend.

It was not only the flashy glasses that attracted attention. RODENSTOCK, a long-established German company of solid quality, produced many popular models, including the brow-type RICHARD, released in 1968, and by the 1970s had manufactured and sold as many as five million frames. In Japan, the heavy brow type with a retro Showa-era look was also popular. The material of the metal frame has also changed. The suspension of the exchange of dollars for gold, announced by President Nixon in 1971, caused the price of gold to soar. Gold-filled, which predictably used a large amount of gold, disappeared, and gold-plating, which applies a thin film of gold, became the norm.

1970s

New Materials Allow Glasses to Increase in Size

Ray-Ban
[OUTDOORSMAN AmberMatic]

1970s, United States
24K Gold Electroplating

The aviator-type OUTDOORSMAN is equipped with the "AmberMatic" all-weather sunglass lens, introduced in 1974. The color of the lens adapts in response to UV rays and other conditions, changing to an orange tone for increased contrast indoors and at nighttime, dark brown on sunny days with high temperatures, and gray on sunny days with low temperatures.

Ray-Ban
[VAGABOND]

1970s, United States
Acetate

Commemorative model of the Ray-Ban
Olympic Games Series, officially recognized
by the US Olympic Committee. The teardrop
sunglasses sport the Olympic logo on the
temples. The retro yellow and orange colors
truly evoke the mood of the '70s.

Persol
[802]

1970s, Italy
Acetate

A large teardrop lens with three lenses that appear to have "three eyes." It is equipped with "meflecto," a bendable temple with a metal cylinder embedded in it, and despite the large shape and massive design, comfort has been carefully taken into consideration.

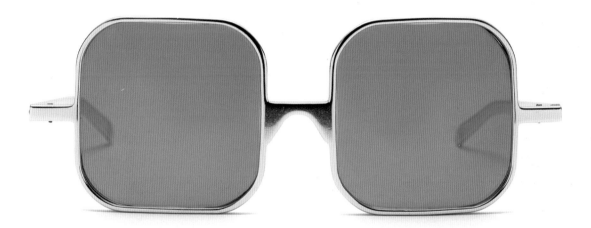

RENAULD

<u>1970s</u>, <u>France</u>
<u>Aluminum</u>

The frame, with its innovative square form with dropped corners, is made of aluminum. The metallic aluminum texture, linear design, and dark-blue lenses create a space-like vibe. Incidentally, RENAULD is a French brand started in 1961 with frame manufacturing done in the United States.

Christian Dior
[D06]

<u>1970s</u>, <u>France</u>
<u>Optyl</u>

Iconic sunglasses made of optyl material. Because it is lightweight, it can be molded into a variety of shapes and can express vivid colors with a beautiful luster; a great deal of decorative eyewear was created from it in the 1970s. The frame is large enough to protrude from the face and can also be sculpted with a hollowed-out frame.

Silhouette
[FUTURA]

<u>1970s</u>, <u>Austria</u>
<u>Acetate</u>

Silhouette released FUTURA in 1974
in limited quantities, a groundbreaking
collection that was the brainchild of eyewear
designer Dora Demel. The futuristic design
with vivid colors and extremely thick frames,
which covered the face, made a big splash and
was also a favorite choice of Elton John.

SWAN

<u>1970s</u>, <u>United States</u>
<u>Aluminum</u>

Square with a double bridge in aluminum.
Aluminum material tends to give an inorganic
and cold impression, but the matte-brown
coloring creates a soft and modern image. The
thick, low-spring nature of these lenses made
them "hard to fit," but this was also part of
their flavor.

United States
Safety Service
[S9]

1970s, United States
Acetate

These include frames that were standardized by the US military and issued to retired military personnel and others. At the time, people still had the image of "glasses = fussy," so they were nicknamed BCG (birth control glasses), meaning that wearing them would make one unattractive.

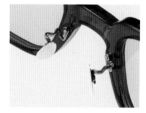

RODENSTOCK
[RICHARD]

1970s, Germany
Acetate, 1/20 12K Gold Filled

RICHARD is a historical model representing the long-established German brand RODENSTOCK. The rugged, thick brow-type combination became very popular in Japan during the Showa period. The design was so well loved that the acetate was later replaced with tortoiseshell for the Japanese market.

MASUNAGA KOKI
[GENTRY-27]

1970s, Japan
Celluloid, 12K Gold Filled

The brow type was created by Masunaga Optical, which was founded in Fukui, Japan, in 1905. It is a massive design with sharp engraving on the voluminous celluloid and a thick metal bridge with 12-karat gold filling. The celluloid temples are clear colored on the inside, allowing the core metal inside to show through.

MASUNAGA KOKI
[EXCEL-205]

1970s, Japan
Celluloid, 12K Gold Filled

Combination brow for women with 12-karat gold-filled metal frame and sturdy celluloid. The rounded shape and soft-brown color are unique, and details such as the perfectly overlapping temple joints show the high quality of made-in-Japan technology.

renoma
[25-201]

<u>1970s</u>, <u>France</u>
<u>Copper Nickel Alloy</u>

From the 1960s onward, the double-bridge design became popular not only for sunglasses, but also for eyeglass frames, with the size of these frames growing even larger in the 1970s. The slightly chunky metal teardrop was the mainstream style of the time, and the all-black, subdued color looks incredible.

Chapter 7

Hip-hop and street culture were at their height in the 1980s. Eyewear became more decorative and bolder in style. A representative example is the German CAZAL, with its large frame and ornate decoration. CAZAL was a preferred brand by many Black artists such as Michael Jackson and M. C. Hammer in the '80s and became a go-to look among many young Black people. The popularity finally heated up so much that a murder occurred in the Bronx, New York, over a pair of CAZALs. It was during this period that specialized eyeglass brands began to emerge. French designer Alain Mikli presented many avant-garde designs, such as asymmetry and mask shapes. He brought the profession of eyewear designer into the mainstream. In the United States, OLIVER PEOPLES was founded in 1987 and began digging up vintage frames from the past.

In the 1980s, a time of economic growth and financial prosperity in many countries, more-playful and more-stylish eyewear made their appearance. ANGLO AMERICAN EYEWEAR in the UK became a hit with its unique designs, such as frogs and clowns, which were like party jokes. On the other hand, Cartier and SEIKO were also introducing luxury eyewear made of the finest materials for the Japanese bubble economy market. Driven by the mood of the times, a wide variety of eyewear appeared in the 1980s. In 1983 the first titanium eyeglasses were successfully commercialized in Japan. Since then, the main material for metal frames has shifted to titanium.

1980s

Decorative and Daring

CAZAL
[616]

1980s, Germany
Acetate, Gold Plated

CAZAL became an icon of hip-hop and street culture in the '80s, when it was used by Black artists. The 616, with its big shape and voluminous square, is a historical model known for being worn by Spike Lee when he appeared in an Air Jordan commercial.

CAZAL
[862]

1980s, West Germany
Acetate

Sharp teardrops with an eye-catching straight brow line typical of the German brand. The turquoise-blue-and-silver brow has a strong presence, and the gold hardware on the temples and the CAZAL logo add a gorgeous touch.

Cartier
[VENDOME SANTOS]

1980s, France
22K Gold Plated

Cartier started its eyewear line in 1983. Frames are inspected with a loupe just as when crafting its jewelry, and a beautiful finish is achieved through high-precision polishing. VENDOME SANTOS is inspired by the world's first wristwatch, the "Santos," and is decorated with the same screw motif as the watch.

Silhouette
[3038/10]

1980s, Austria
Acetate

Silhouette had a strong affinity with hip-hop and Black culture in the 1980s. The asymmetrical, avant-garde design was well complemented by the red-and-white pop coloring. The temples were red and white with different colors on the left and right sides and were decorated with an "S" logo.

alain mikli
[CLÉ DE SOL]

1980s, France
Acetate

The design that made alain mikli's name known around the world was CLÉ DE SOL. The unique eyewear, reminiscent of a musical note, was created for the Claude Montana show, and only 20 pieces were produced worldwide. In 1982, Andy Warhol wore it and it became the talk of the town.

PORSCHE DESIGN
by CARRERA
[5621]

1980s, Austria
Nickel Alloy

A collaboration between CARRERA, founded by world-renowned eyeglass developer Wilhelm Unger, and PORSCHE DESIGN. The large teardrops feature a "lens interchangeable system" that allows the wearer to change lenses simply by pulling up the clip on the bridge.

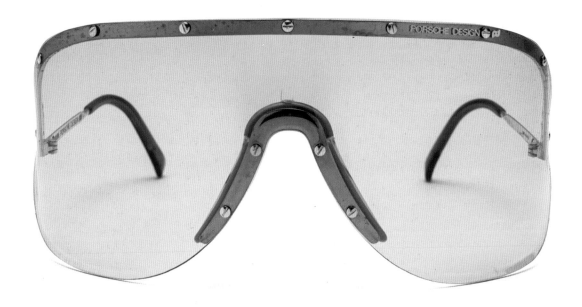

PORSCHE DESIGN
by CARRERA
[5620]

1980s, Austria
Polycarbonate, Nickel Alloy

This legendary model was worn by Yoko
Ono on the cover of *Rolling Stone* and was
also used by Stevie Wonder. These shield-
type sunglasses, which cover the face, have
one-piece lenses for a wide field of vision.
Lightweight polycarbonate material makes
even larger shapes light and durable.

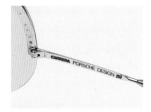

BOEING CARRERA
[5701]

1980s, Austria
Nickel Alloy

A collaboration between American aircraft maker BOEING and CARRERA. Matte black metal. The teardrops are accented with the red "CARRERA" logo and lines on the temples. It is functional, with spring hinges that allow the temples to open in the opposite direction.

PLAYBOY
[4558]

1980s, United States
Optyl

PLAYBOY, an American adult entertainment company, introduced eyewear made of optyl material in the 1980s. As in the magazine, the design was characterized by sexiness and humor, and on the temples was the profile of a rabbit wearing a bow tie, the unmistakable Playboy "Rabbit Head." Manufacturing was done in Germany.

ANGLO AMERICAN EYEWEAR
[frog]

1980s, United Kingdom
Acetate

Founded in England in 1882, ANGLO AMERICAN EYEWEAR has created many unique eyewear products. "frog" has a cute design with two frogs facing each other, but the droopy-eyed lens shape makes it look a bit strange when worn. The temple ends are frog legs, which is a fine device.

Persol
[649]

1980s, Italy
Acetate

Conceived to protect streetcar drivers from wind and dust, 649 featured silver arrow decoration and "meflecto" temples that curved to fit the shape of the face. It is a masterpiece representing Persol. Steve McQueen wore the 649 foldable in the 1968 film *The Thomas Crown Affair*.

Persol
[001]

<u>1980s</u>, <u>Italy</u>
<u>Acetate</u>

These bold sunglasses, with glass lenses on both sides of the front like a windshield, also reduce the glare of light coming around from the sides. Decorative eyewear was a hot topic in the 1980s, and Persol, a well-established sunglass brand, also introduced some quirky designs during this period.

dunhill
[6056]

1980s, United Kingdom
Gold Plated, Buffalo Horn

The metal frames of the British royal warrant brand Dunhill incorporated a wheat ear pattern, just like the highly popular lighter "ROLLA GAS." It was a special version with buffalo horns on the brow line and was manufactured in Germany. "GENUINE HORN TRIMS" is engraved on the temples.

SEIKO VISTA
[LION D'OR]

1980s, Japan
18K Solid Gold

SEIKO started its own eyeglasses brand, VISTA, in 1973. In the 1980s, under the name LION D'OR (Golden Lion), the company introduced a luxurious collection using 18-karat gold and genuine tortoiseshell. Luxurious frames made with high-grade materials and advanced technology were made possible because of the roaring bubble economy.

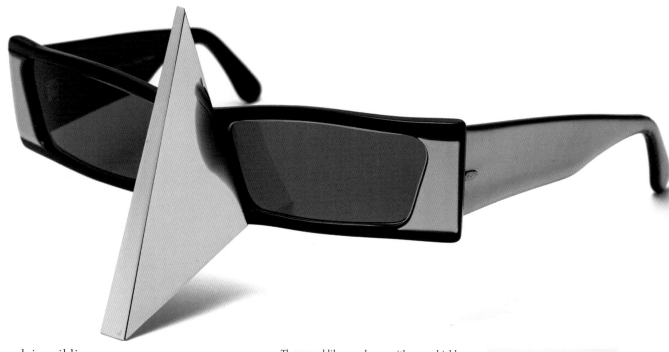

alain mikli
[A.M.88]

<u>1980s</u>, <u>France</u>
<u>Acetate</u>
<u>Nickel Copper Alloy</u>

These masklike sunglasses with nose shields are a parody of alain mikli's own nose, which was also used in the 1987 advertising visuals. The avant-garde design, which showcases alain mikli's creativity, was reissued in 2014.

alain mikli
[637]

<u>1980s</u>, <u>France</u>
<u>Acetate</u>, <u>Alloy</u>

The combination model with a double bridge and demipatterned acetate showed alain mikli's progressive spirit with an artistic design that was also suitable for daily use. The horizontal square shape and straight brow line were an innovative touch, and the matte black gave it a fashionable feel.

ROBERT LA ROCHE
[543]

1980s, Austria
Acetate, Alloy

Combination frames from ROBERT LA ROCHE, a designer brand founded in Austria in 1973. While incorporating polygonal lens shapes that were common in vintage frames from around the 1920s, the rounded, beveled metal temples created a playful look.

lafont.
PARIS

Traitement sans nickel
Nickel - free coating

Lafont Paris

<u>1980s</u>, <u>France</u>
<u>Nickel Alloy</u>, <u>Acetate</u>

Lafont began as an optician in Paris in 1923, and the eyeglasses brand was later founded in 1979. Its "Crown Panto," a traditional French design, had a metallic-green frame with a beautifully patterned acetate reminiscent of a peacock. The temples were stamped "JEAN LAFONT," the second generation of the Lafont family.

MASUNAGA KOKI
[CONTINENTAL]

1980s, Japan
Nickel Chrome Alloy

High-quality square shape that is a product of Japanese craftsmanship. The double structure of the metal rim, with a voluminous brow at the top, is accented by a three-dimensional bridge. The brow was matte-finished and the rim was mirror-finished to give the design and texture a more distinctive look.

MASUNAGA KOKI
[METAL 126]

1980s, Japan
Nickel Chrome Alloy

The large square shape and the double bridge, which gave the glasses a slightly unrefined impression, represented the mood of Japanese eyeglasses in the Showa period (1926–89). The straight bar bridge not only was a design point but also served to maintain the strength of the frame.

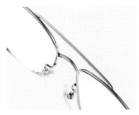

OLIVER PEOPLES
[OP-78]

1980s, United States
Nickel Alloy

Inspired by vintage American frames, OLIVER PEOPLES was born in 1987. The OP-78, introduced early on, followed the FUL-VUE style popular in the '30s and the cable temples of the past. It was manufactured in Japan and has intricate engraving.

OLIVER PEOPLES
[OP-LE]

1980s, United States
Nickel Alloy

The OP-LE has a round shape, almost like
a regular circle, incorporating a U-shaped
bridge reminiscent of American Optical's
"CORTLAND." The frame has a coin-edged
engraving, which, combined with the antique
gold color, creates a stately atmosphere.
"FRAME JAPAN" is engraved on the temples.

Chapter 8

In the 1990s, luxury brands and licensed eyewear makers were in a honeymoon phase, and the market was flooded with wonderful masterpieces. JEAN PAUL GAULTIER's eyewear manufactured in Japan was particularly outstanding. The intricate Eiffel Tower motif design and elaborate steampunk-inspired details incorporating parts of industrial goods could not have been realized without Japan's advanced metalworking technology. At the time, GIORGIO ARMANI, GIANNI VERSACE, and GIANFRANCO FERRE were known as the "3Gs of Milan," and mode brands were at their peak.

In eyewear, the brand's logo and marks were boldly displayed, a unique approach that could only be seen in the 1990s.

On the other hand, also in the 1990s, the performance of plastic lenses such as progressive lenses continued to evolve, enabling even small frames to provide a more comfortable field of vision than previously seen. As a result, smart square and oval shapes with shallower top and bottom widths than before became popular new designs. In addition, modern eyewear that eliminated waste and featured lightweight materials such as titanium and unique screwless hinges, led by Denmark's LINDBERGE, became the forefront of the era. At this point, eyewear had distanced itself from fashion trends and entered an era in which eyewear was differentiated by individual frames, such as hinges and other unique mechanisms, complex and difficult forms, and lightweight frames.

1990s

Made in Japan: Technical Capabilities

JEAN PAUL GAULTIER
[Eiffel tower]

1990s, France
Nickel Alloy

Manufactured with advanced Japanese technology, JEAN PAUL GAULTIER glasses are an essential part of the history of eyewear in the 1990s. As the model name suggests, the Eiffel tower is an innovative design inspired by the steel structure of the Eiffel Tower. The complex "truss structure" of connecting triangles is beautifully expressed.

MATSUDA
[10611]

1990s, Japan
Titanium

MATSUDA is an eyewear line launched by
the late Mitsuhiro Matsuda, founder of the
DC brand NICOLE, for the international
market in 1989. These ornate sunglasses with
D-shaped lenses and side guards were inspired
by antique frames from the 1800s.

KENZO
[KE 2894]

1990s, Japan
Acetate

These small, oval-shaped sunglasses had a bold KENZO logo with a metallic-blue plate matching the top of the front. The technique of large brand logos was one of the popular styles in the 1990s. It is interesting that the expression changes depending on the angle of view.

GIORGIO ARMANI
[121]

<u>1990s</u>, <u>Italy</u>
<u>Nickel Copper Alloy</u>

GIORGIO ARMANI has gained popularity for
his method of reconstructing classic styles in
a modern way, and this stance has remained
consistent in eyewear as well. The round shape,
which is close to a regular circle, is combined
with a double bridge and finished smartly with
beautiful lines and matte silver color.

l.a. Eyeworks
[pluto II]

1990s, United States
Aluminum

Born in Los Angeles in 1979, l.a. Eyeworks is a brand that led the eyewear scene in the 1990s with its artistic frames. The pluto II has a complex structure with metal rims and a flowing brow and bars, creating a unique grasshopper-like shape.

CUTLER AND GROSS

[0568]

1990s, United Kingdom
Acetate

Founded in London in 1969, Cutler and Gross introduced a number of experimental designs in the 1990s. These sunglasses with a hollowed-out front and triple-bridge expression, combined with the right-angled bend of the front, created a "classic car" look.

JEAN PAUL GAULTIER
[56-5109]

<u>1990s</u>, <u>France</u>
<u>Nickel Copper Alloy</u>

With metallic-blue springs on the brow line
and rail lines on the bridge and temples,
this ambitious work incorporates parts of
industrial products as motifs. JEAN PAUL
GAULTIER's signature steampunk style
conveys a sense of the '90s.

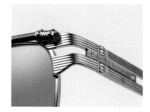

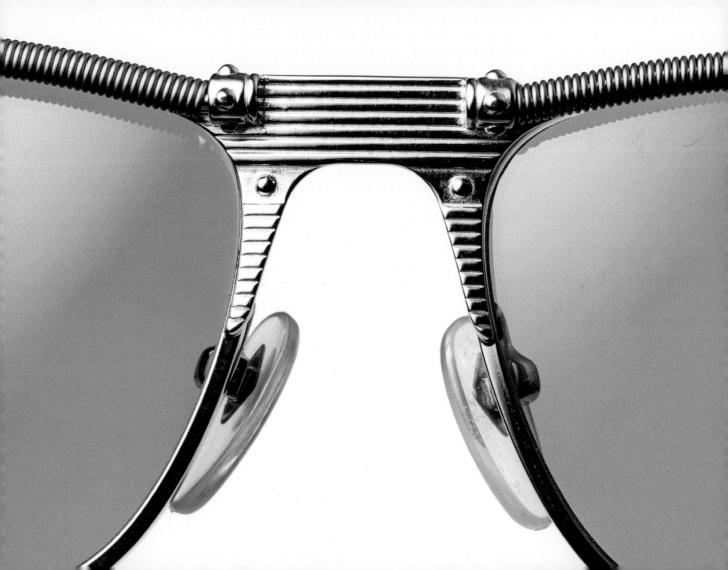

JUNIOR GAULTIER
[58-0105]

1990s, France
Nickel Copper Alloy

The second line of JUNIOR GAULTIER, which existed from 1988 to 1994, was a novel round shape with four lenses. The side lenses are folded inward to fit perfectly with the front lenses; this playful and intricate design was achieved with precise Japanese processing technology.

OPTICAL AFFAIRS
[6558]

1990s, United States
Acetate

Legendary white sunglasses worn by late Nirvana singer Kurt Cobain. The oversized oval cat's-eyes with extremely thick rims were reminiscent of the 1960s. OPTICAL AFFAIRS is the predecessor of popular New York eyewear brand Christian Roth.

GIANFRANCO FERRE
[GFF77]

1990s, Italy
Gold Plated

GIANFRANCO FERRE is known as one of the "3Gs of Milan," along with GIANNI VERSACE and GIORGIO ARACE, and is a brand that has led the fashion scene. The half-moon-shaped sunglasses in brilliant yellow gold were gorgeous with crystals on the front.

YVES SAINT LAURENT
[5014]

1990s, France
Acetate

These cat's-eye-shaped sunglasses were black and gold with a luxurious color scheme. The metal parts on the front were of a massive design reminiscent of ancient Egypt. The YVES SAINT LAURENT logo on the outside of the temples was also a key feature.

GIANNI VERSACE
[MOD 420/C]

1990s, Italy
Nickel Alloy

Sunglasses with stunning impact featuring GIANNI VERSACE's gold Medusa symbol on the ultrathick temples. This MOD 420/C is also known as the favorite of Notorious B.I.G., an American rapper who was assassinated in 1997 at the young age of 24.

Ray-Ban

<u>1990s</u>, <u>United States</u>
<u>24K Electroplating</u>

The last model manufactured by Bausch&Lomb before Ray-Ban was acquired by Italian company Luxottica in 1999. These high-curved sunglasses are reminiscent of the "Yankee style" of the '90s, with their extremely raised lens shape and low height.

OLIVER PEOPLES
[OP-662]

1990s, United States
Unknown

The square shape with little height is an under-rim-type reading glass. It is interesting to see how the '90s incorporated classic vintage frame construction, such as saddle bridges without nose pads and sliding temples with adjustable lengths.

LINDBERG
[AIR TITANIUM]

1990s, Denmark
Titanium

Founded in 1985, LINDBERG used the highest grade of pure titanium to develop ultralightweight glasses without screws or brazing. The originator of the minimalist design without screws, the rimless frames, introduced about 30 years ago, are still a universal product that feels timeless.

100 Years in the Production Area of Glasses in Japan

This book introduces vintage eyeglasses from the 1920s to the 1990s, but what path did Japanese eyeglasses take during that period? Japan's leading eyeglass production center is Fukui Prefecture, centered in the city of Sabae, which commands a domestic market share of over 90%. The eyeglass industry was born in Fukui in 1905. Fukui is a cold region, and in winter the city is isolated by deep snowfall. In response, Gozaemon Masunaga, a village councilor at the time, invited eyeglass makers from Osaka and started eyeglass production in his hometown of Ikuno (now Fukui City) so that farmers could have a side job during the off-season.

Fukui's eyeglass industry has developed new technologies while adapting to global trends and fashions. For example, in the mid-1920s, large numbers of gold-filled frames, known as "Beikin" (meaning American gold), were imported from the United States. To stop the "Beikin" offensive, Kikujiro Kimura, a metal-plating business owner in Fukui City, acquired equipment from Germany and, after studying with specialist craftsmen in Osaka, perfected his own gold-plating and gold-filling processes. At the same time, movie actor Harold Lloyd appeared on screen wearing celluloid round glasses, which became a big hit in Japan. At that time,

1: In Fukui Prefecture, a "mecca for opticians," you will occasionally see objects made of glasses. 2: The "choba system" in practice at the Masunaga plant. The craftsmen were asked to make eyeglasses in groups, and their skills were honed by having them compete against each other to see who could make the best pair of glasses, further motivating them.

1 2

craftsman Suekichi Sasaki obtained celluloid materials in Osaka and invented the "Modern," as it was commonly known in Japan, in which celluloid is wrapped around the temple ends. Subsequently, many celluloid frames were manufactured in Fukui.

The reason for the development of eyeglass-manufacturing technology in Fukui can be attributed to the "choba system," adopted by Gozaemon Masunaga. Under this system, master craftsmen, artisans, and apprentices manufacture eyeglasses in groups called "choba," and train apprentices while competing on technique and cost. The Sabae area became the center of the eyeglass

industry, as skilled craftsmen established themselves in the area. After the war, demand for eyeglasses surged amid rapid economic growth, and the region captured a 95% share of the Japanese market in the mid-1970s. They actively sought overseas sales channels, and by this time they were exporting approximately 60% of the eyeglasses they produced.

A turning point later came when the Japanese name became recognized around the world. In 1983, companies in Fukui Prefecture succeeded in commercializing the world's first titanium frames. Titanium is 40% lighter than steel and more resistant to rust, yet the hardness of the material

made it a challenge to process. Once Japan became the first country in the world to master titanium-processing technology, well-known foreign brands such as PRADA and GUCCI turned to Japanese companies to manufacture their eyewear. They produced eyewear for JEAN PAUL GAULTIER in the 1990s, embodying the complex designs generated by the designer. Fukui's advanced technology has raised the level of eyeglass design in the world. Thus, along with Italy and China, Japan came to be known as one of the world's three major producers of eyeglasses. Nowadays it is commonplace to see eyewear stamped "Made in Japan" in boutiques overseas.

Appendix 2

Valuable Old Tools for Glasses Collected from All Over the World

The vintage store, which travels around the world to collect frames, displays not only valuable frames, but also optical instruments of the time.

1-2: A 1940s French stamping machine with dies. Glasses were manufactured by mounting a die on a machine and punching out a sheet of acetate. 3: Upper left and lower left are optometry frames from the 1960s. 4: A sign that imitates eyeglasses used in Europe in the 1910s. 5: A compact measuring instrument that measures the curve of a lens to determine the degree of diopter, the refractive power of the lens. 6: Old Chinese spectacles. 7: A three-sided mirror made in Germany. The back of the mirror is the sight chart.

(GLOBE SPECS)

1

2

3

4

5

6

7

Appendix 3

The "Supporting Cast" That Supported the Glasses through the Ages

Catalogs, paper packages, and other
vintage items found in a warehouse
along with the glasses. The colors and
design convey the mood of the time.

1: A box that contained frames more than half a century
old.
2: In the past, eyeglasses were sold in paper sleeve cases.
3: The age and type of frame may be determined from
a 100-year-old price list or other sources. 4: Screws
that can still be used for repairs are extremely rare. 5:
A feminine eyeglass chain made over 100 years ago. 6:
Tools from American Optical.

7: Persol sunglass lenses featured in this book. 8:
Valuable outer boxes from TART OPTICAL and
American Optical.

(SOLAKZADE)

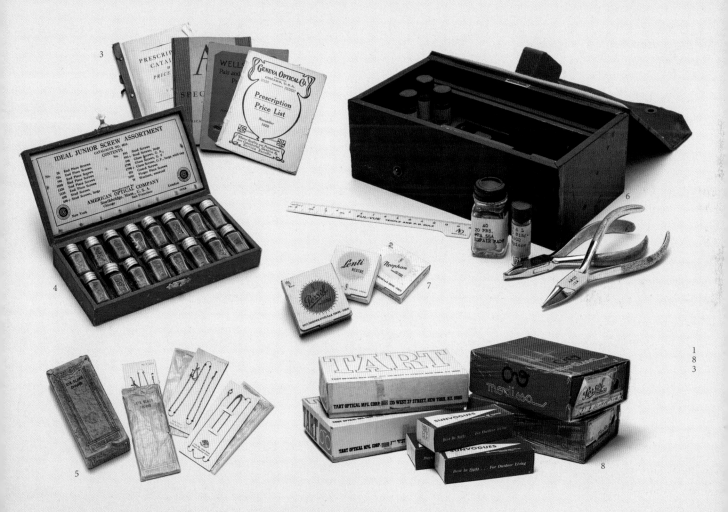

3

183

PRESCRIP
CATALO
a
PRICE

A
SPEC

WELLS
Pair and
P

GENEVA OPTICAL Co.
CHICAGO, U.S.A.

Prescription
Price List

November
1909

IDEAL JUNIOR SCREW ASSORTMENT
CATALOGUE NO. 4616
CONTENTS

AMERICAN OPTICAL COMPANY
Southbridge, Mass., U.S.A.

4

6

7

FUL-VUE

5

8

TART

TART OPTICAL MFG. CORP.

medimal

SUNVOGUES

Appendix 4

What Is the Appeal behind the Glass Lens, an Item Rarely Seen Today?

Until about half a century ago, lenses for eyeglasses were mostly made of glass. More than 95% of eyeglass lenses today utilize plastic lenses. The relationship between glass and plastic lenses is similar to the change in drink containers from glass bottles to plastic. Glass bottles are beautiful in color and have a nice look but are heavy and can break if dropped. Recyclable PET bottles are light, easy to carry, and difficult to break. The same can be said for eyeglass lenses. Glass lenses are scratch resistant and maintain clear vision. Due to the fact that they don't fade under ultraviolet light, they are also resistant to deterioration over time. Some disadvantages are that they are heavier than plastic lenses, break easily, and require more time and effort to process. Plastic lenses, on the other hand, are lightweight and break resistant and can be used with a wide variety of frames. The disadvantages are that they are susceptible to heat and scratching and will yellow over time. Although the shift to easy-to-handle plastic lenses was a trend of the times, many fans still prefer the higher quality of glass lenses. That is why even today, top eyewear brands, especially in the US, dare to use glass for their sunglass lenses.

Appendix 5

Vintage Glasses:
Simple Q&A

Q1. How to recognize vintage glasses that are in good condition

Over time, plastic frames may shrink due to the loss of plasticizers, a liquid substance used in manufacturing plastic, as well as other moisture. Careful attention should especially be paid to Sirmont and "celluloid-wrapped" pieces, since the material can shrink and become shorter in length. Some old plastic frames may have a sour smell. This smell cannot be removed, so check well. Also check for loose rivet fittings and hinges.

Q2. How do I find the right frame?

Pay attention to the size, since many vintage European and American pieces have a smaller front width. It is advisable to choose a pair of glasses that, when worn, position the eyes in the middle or slightly inward in the front.

Q3. Can prescription lenses be put in vintage frames?

Prescription lenses can usually be installed, but it will depend on lens condition, so you should check with the store first.

Q4. Are vintage glasses expensive?

Some of them come with a premium and cost more than $2,200, but if you look for them, you can find affordable ones in the $215 range.

Q5. Where is the charm in owning vintage glasses?

Manufacturing methods and materials differ from country to country and period to period, giving the glasses a unique presence not found in today's eyewear. Because they are one-of-a-kind items for which there is no substitute, they are also recommended for those who prefer something that sets them apart.

Q6. What precautions should be taken when handling vintage pieces?

Moisture and oil are very harmful, so be sure to wipe off sweat, for instance, after wearing them. Store the glasses in a stable and dry environment after use.

Q7. What should I do when my glasses slip off?

You should never attempt to repair modern eyeglasses by yourself, much less vintage models. Buy from a specialty store that can adjust or repair them and have them adjusted in the store.

Glossary

● **attaching**

To tightly attach the joints of fixtures and other equipment with a specialized tool. In the case of glasses, they are secured by rivets on the hinges.

● **aviator**

Pilot sunglasses developed by Ray-Ban in the 1930s at the request of the US Air Force.

● **Bakelite**

The world's first fully synthetic plastic, created in 1909. It was used for nose pads and other materials.

● **cable temple**

The temples, which wrap around the back of the ear, were developed by American Optical in 1885 for equestrian use.

● **celluloid-wrapped**

Refers to a thin plastic wrapped around a metal rim. The name came from the fact that it was wrapped in celluloid.

● **counterbore**

Carving the plastic material so that it does not pop out of the face of the plastic material when the hinge is installed.

● **fat temple**

Extra-thick temples made of celluloid that retain their strength even without a core. Often used in French vintage.

● **full view**

The design with the temples positioned at the top. Developed by American Optical in 1930.

● **injection molding**

A molding method in which plastic melted by heat is injected into a mold, which cools and solidifies.

● **newmont**

A method developed by American Optical in the 1930s to secure rimless frames at a single point.

● **rimless**

Refers to spectacles without a rim surrounding the lenses. It was developed by American Optical in 1874.

● **rimway**

Refers to a method of fastening rimless frames at two points, with the metal rim along the lens.

Finally, we will introduce some terms that were not fully explained in this volume. Some terms are specific to vintage and should also be used as a reference when making a purchase.

● rivet

A tack that is inserted into a member with a hole and swaged or attached to secure it. In eyeglasses it is mainly used to fix hinges.

● saddle bridge

A bridge without nose pads, curved so that it rests on the nose. In Japan it is also called "Ichiyama style."

● side mount

Design style with temples placed from the center of the front side. It was common before 1930.

● temple end

The tip of the temple. The cover of the earpiece part made of plastic or other material is called "Modern" in Japan.

● tortoiseshell

A processed product of the shell of the hawksbill turtle, a type of sea turtle. It is a natural material that has been used for glasses and combs since ancient times.

● with/without a core

With or without a core embedded in the temples. Some robust celluloid can retain its strength without a core.

References

Eyewear: A Visual History
Moss Lipow
Taschen GmbH | 2011

Spectacles & Sunglasses
Pepin | 2006

Fashions in Eyeglasses: From the Fourteenth Century to Present Day
Richard Corson
Humanities Press | 1980

Fashion Spectacles, Spectacular Fashion
Simon Murray & Nicky Albrechtsen
Thames & Hudson | 2012

Full-Fledged Eyewear Compendium
Sekaibunka Holdings | 2020

Index

1920s ▷

P18 | SE   P19 | SZ   P20 | SE   P21 | SE   P22 | SZ   P24 | SZ   P25 | SE

P26SZ   P27 | SZ   P28 | SZ   P29 | SE   P30 | SZ   P31 | SZ   P32 | GS   P33 | SZ

P34 | SZ   1930s ▷   P38 | SZ   P39 | GS   P40 | SZ   P41 | SZ   P42 | SZ   P44 | SE

P45 | SE   P46 | SZ   P47 | SZ   P48 | SZ   P50 | SZ   P51 | SZ   1940s ▷   P54 | SE

P55SE   P56 | SE   P58 | SE   P59 | SE   P60 | SE   P61 | SE   P62 | SZ   P63 | GS

List of glasses in this book. The page number and the store where they can found are clearly indicated.

P64 | SZ   P66 | GS   P67 | SZ   P68 | SZ   P69 | SZ   P70 | SZ   1950s ▷   P74 | SZ

P75 | SZ   P76 | SZ   P78 | SZ   P79 | SZ   P80 | GS   P81 | GS   P82 | SZ   P84 | GS

P85 | SZ   P86 | GS   P87 | SZ   P88 | SZ   P89 | SZ   P90 | SE   P91 | GS   1960s ▷

P94 | SZ   P95 | SE   P96 | SE   P98SE   P99 | GS   P100 | SE   P101 | SE   P102 | SZ

P103 | SZ   P104 | SZ   P105 | SZ   P106 | SZ   P107 | SZ   P108 | SZ   P110 | SZ   P111 | SZ

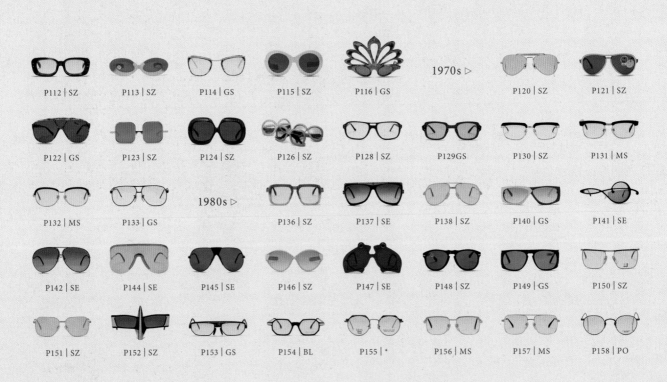

P112 | SZ   P113 | SZ   P114 | GS   P115 | SZ   P116 | GS   1970s ▷   P120 | SZ   P121 | SZ

P122 | GS   P123 | SZ   P124 | SZ   P126 | SZ   P128 | SZ   P129GS   P130 | SZ   P131 | MS

P132 | MS   P133 | GS   1980s ▷   P136 | SZ   P137 | SE   P138 | SZ   P140 | GS   P141 | SE

P142 | SE   P144 | SE   P145 | SE   P146 | SZ   P147 | SE   P148 | SZ   P149 | GS   P150 | SZ

P151 | SZ   P152 | SZ   P153 | GS   P154 | BL   P155 | *   P156 | MS   P157 | MS   P158 | PO

Shop

P159 | PO

1990s ▷

P162 | SE

P163 | SZ

P164 | SZ

P165 | SZ

P166 | SE

P167 | BL

P168 | SZ

P170 | SZ

P171 | SE

P172 | SZ

P173 | SZ

P174 | SZ

P175 | SZ

P176 | PO

P177 | GS

SOLAKZADE
4-29-4 Jingumae, Shibuya-ku, Tokyo
150-0001
Tel: 03-3478-3345

GLOBE SPECS
[Shibuya Branch]
1-7-9 Jinnan, Shibuya-ku, Tokyo
150-0041
Tel: 03-5459-8377

SPEAKEASY
[Kobe Headquarters]
2F, 2-13-8 Nakayamate-dori,
Chuo-ku, Kobe-shi, Hyogo 650-0004
Tel: 078-855-5759

PonMegane
[Urawa Branch]
3-6-9 Takasago, Urawa-ku, Saita-
ma-shi, Saitama 330-0063
Tel: 048-762-3919

blinc
2-27-20, Minami-Aoyama, Mina-
to-ku, Tokyo 107-0062
Tel: 03-5775-7525

www.vintageframescompany.com
www.eyeglasseswarehouse.com
vintageopticalshop.com
edandsarna.com

SOLAKZADE® GLOBE SPECS SPEAKEASY ponmegane blinc

Takano Fujii

Spectacle writer. After graduating from university, he worked for an editing production company before becoming a freelancer. He comes in contact with more than 1,000 pairs of glasses a year and writes articles on all kinds of eyewear, including at trade fairs, factories, and product introductions in Japan and abroad. He is in charge of programming and advisor for eyeglasses specials on TV, such as *The World Is Full of Things I Want* and *The Coming and Going Times—Heisei Last-Day Special*. He also shares the appeal of eyeglasses on his website and YouTube channel.

English-edition copyright © 2024 by Schiffer Publishing, Ltd.

Library of Congress Control Number: 2024932161

All rights reserved. No part of this work may be reproduced or used in any form or by any means—graphic, electronic, or mechanical, including photocopying or information storage and retrieval systems—without written permission from the publisher.

The scanning, uploading, and distribution of this book or any part thereof via the Internet or any other means without the permission of the publisher is illegal and punishable by law. Please purchase only authorized editions and do not participate in or encourage the electronic piracy of copyrighted materials.

"Schiffer," "Schiffer Publishing, Ltd.," and the pen and inkwell logo are registered trademarks of Schiffer Publishing, Ltd.

ISBN:978-0-7643-6753-3

Printed in India

Published by Schiffer Publishing, Ltd.
4880 Lower Valley Road
Atglen, PA 19310
Phone: (610) 593-1777; Fax: (610) 593-2002
Email: info@schifferbooks.com
Web: www.schifferbooks.com

For our complete selection of fine books on this and related subjects, please visit our website at www.schifferbooks.com. You may also write for a free catalog. Schiffer Publishing's titles are available at special discounts for bulk purchases for sales promotions or premiums. Special editions,including personalized covers, corporate imprints, and excerpts, can be created in large quantities for special needs. For more information, contact the publisher.

We are always looking for people to write books on new and related subjects. If you have an idea for a book, please contact us at proposals@schifferbooks.com.

VINTAGE EYEWARE STYLE: 1920s–1990s

by Takano Fujii
© 2021 Takano Fujii
© 2021 GRAPHIC-sha PUBLISHING CO., LTD
First designed and published in Japan in 2021 by Graphic-sha Publishing Co., Ltd.
English edition published in the United States of America in 2024 by Schiffer Publishing, Ltd.
English translation rights arranged with Graphic-sha Publishing Co., Ltd. through Japan UNI Agency, Inc., Tokyo

Original edition creative staff
Book design: Takuya Kawashima / Koto Otawa (Kawashima Office)
Photos: Tatsuya Ozawa (Studio Mug)
Planning collaborator: Miho Obara (translation)
Editorial collaboration: Ouraidou K.K.
Special Thanks: SOLAKZADE / GLOBE SPECS / SPEAKEASY / pon megane / blinc Masunaga Optical Mfg. Co., Ltd.
MEGANE MUSEUM
Editing: Hitomi Koga (Graphic-sha Publishing Co., Ltd.)

English edition creative staff
English translation: Yuko Wada, Sean Gaston
English edition layout: Shinichi Ishioka
Foreign edition production and management: Takako Motoki (Graphic-sha Publishing Co., Ltd.)